RECIPE JOURNAL BOOK

YOUR BEST KEPT RECIPES IN THIS BLANK COOKBOOK

Recipe Name:

Date:

Preparation Time:

Servings:

Special Note:

Ingredients:

Directions:

Recipe Name:

Date:

Preparation Time:

Servings:

Special Note:

Ingredients:

Directions:

Recipe Name:

Date:

Preparation Time:

Servings:

Special Note:

Ingredients:

Directions:

Recipe Name:

Date:

Preparation Time:

Servings:

Special Note:

Ingredients:

Directions:

Recipe Name:

Date:

Preparation Time:

Servings:

Special Note:

Ingredients:

Directions:

Recipe Name:

Date:

Preparation Time:

Servings:

Special Note:

Ingredients:

Directions:

Recipe Name:

Date:

Preparation Time:

Servings:

Special Note:

Ingredients:

Directions:

Recipe Name:

Date:

Preparation Time:

Servings:

Special Note:

Ingredients:

Directions:

Recipe Name:

Date:

Preparation Time:

Servings:

Special Note:

Ingredients:

-
-
-
-
-
-
-
-
-
-
-
-
-
-
-
-
-
-
-
-

Directions:

Recipe Name:

Date:

Preparation Time:

Servings:

Special Note:

Ingredients:

Directions:

Recipe Name:

Date:

Preparation Time:

Servings:

Special Note:

Ingredients:

Directions:

Recipe Name:

Date:

Preparation Time:

Servings:

Special Note:

Ingredients:

Directions:

Recipe Name:

Date:

Preparation Time:

Servings:

Special Note:

Ingredients:

Directions:

Recipe Name:

Date:

Preparation Time:

Servings:

Special Note:

Ingredients:

Directions:

Recipe Name:

Date:

Preparation Time:

Servings:

Special Note:

Ingredients:

-
-
-
-
-
-
-
-
-
-
-
-
-
-
-
-
-
-
-
-

Directions:

Recipe Name:

Date:

Preparation Time:

Servings:

Special Note:

Ingredients:

-
-
-
-
-
-
-
-
-
-
-
-
-
-
-
-
-
-
-
-

Directions:

Recipe Name:

Date:

Preparation Time:

Servings:

Special Note:

Ingredients:

Directions:

Recipe Name:

Date:

Preparation Time:

Servings:

Special Note:

Ingredients:

Directions:

Recipe Name:

Date:

Preparation Time:

Servings:

Special Note:

Ingredients:

•
•
•
•
•
•
•
•
•
•
•
•
•
•
•
•
•
•
•
•

Directions:

Recipe Name:

Date:

Preparation Time:

Servings:

Special Note:

Ingredients:

Directions:

Recipe Name:

Date:

Preparation Time:

Servings:

Special Note:

Ingredients:

Directions:

Recipe Name:

Date:

Preparation Time:

Servings:

Special Note:

Ingredients:

Directions:

Recipe Name:

Date:

Preparation Time:

Servings:

Special Note:

Ingredients:

•
•
•
•
•
•
•
•
•
•
•
•
•
•
•
•
•
•
•
•

Directions:

Recipe Name:

Date:

Preparation Time:

Servings:

Special Note:

Ingredients:

•
•
•
•
•
•
•
•
•
•
•
•
•
•
•
•
•
•
•
•

Directions:

Recipe Name:

Date:

Preparation Time:

Servings:

Special Note:

Ingredients:

Directions:

Recipe Name:

Date:

Preparation Time:

Servings:

Special Note:

Ingredients:

Directions:

Recipe Name:

Date:

Preparation Time:

Servings:

Special Note:

Ingredients:

-
-
-
-
-
-
-
-
-
-
-
-
-
-
-
-
-
-
-
-

Directions:

Recipe Name:

Date:

Preparation Time:

Servings:

Special Note:

Ingredients:

Directions:

Recipe Name:

Date:

Preparation Time:

Servings:

Special Note:

Ingredients:

Directions:

Recipe Name:

Date:

Preparation Time:

Servings:

Special Note:

Ingredients:

Directions:

Recipe Name:

Date:

Preparation Time:

Servings:

Special Note:

Ingredients:

-
-
-
-
-
-
-
-
-
-
-
-
-
-
-
-
-
-
-
-

Directions:

Recipe Name:

Date:

Preparation Time:

Servings:

Special Note:

Ingredients:

Directions:

Recipe Name:

Date:

Preparation Time:

Servings:

Special Note:

Ingredients:

Directions:

Recipe Name:

Date:

Preparation Time:

Servings:

Special Note:

Ingredients:

Directions:

Recipe Name:

Date:

Preparation Time:

Servings:

Special Note:

Ingredients:

Directions:

Recipe Name:

Date:

Preparation Time:

Servings:

Special Note:

Ingredients:

Directions:

Recipe Name:

Date:

Preparation Time:

Servings:

Special Note:

Ingredients:

-
-
-
-
-
-
-
-
-
-
-
-
-
-
-
-
-
-
-
-

Directions:

Recipe Name:

Date:

Preparation Time:

Servings:

Special Note:

Ingredients:

Directions:

Recipe Name:

Date:

Preparation Time:

Servings:

Special Note:

Ingredients:

Directions:

Recipe Name:

Date:

Preparation Time:

Servings:

Special Note:

Ingredients:

-
-
-
-
-
-
-
-
-
-
-
-
-
-
-
-
-
-
-
-

Directions:

Recipe Name:

Date:

Preparation Time:

Servings:

Special Note:

Ingredients:

Directions:

Recipe Name:

Date:

Preparation Time:

Servings:

Special Note:

Ingredients:

Directions:

Recipe Name:

Date:

Preparation Time:

Servings:

Special Note:

Ingredients:

Directions:

Recipe Name:

Date:

Preparation Time:

Servings:

Special Note:

Ingredients:

Directions:

Recipe Name:

Date:

Preparation Time:

Servings:

Special Note:

Ingredients:

Directions:

Recipe Name:

Date:

Preparation Time:

Servings:

Special Note:

Ingredients:

-
-
-
-
-
-
-
-
-
-
-
-
-
-
-
-
-
-
-
-

Directions:

Recipe Name:

Date:

Preparation Time:

Servings:

Special Note:

Ingredients:

Directions:

Recipe Name:

Date:

Preparation Time:

Servings:

Special Note:

Ingredients:

Directions:

Recipe Name:

Date:

Preparation Time:

Servings:

Special Note:

Ingredients:

-
-
-
-
-
-
-
-
-
-
-
-
-
-
-
-
-
-
-
-

Directions:

Recipe Name:

Date:

Preparation Time:

Servings:

Special Note:

Ingredients:

Directions:

Recipe Name:

Date:

Preparation Time:

Servings:

Special Note:

Ingredients:

Directions:

Recipe Name:

Date:

Preparation Time:

Servings:

Special Note:

Ingredients:

Directions:

Recipe Name:

Date:

Preparation Time:

Servings:

Special Note:

Ingredients:

Directions:

Recipe Name:

Date:

Preparation Time:

Servings:

Special Note:

Ingredients:

Directions:

Recipe Name:

Date:

Preparation Time:

Servings:

Special Note:

Ingredients:

Directions:

Recipe Name:

Date:

Preparation Time:

Servings:

Special Note:

Ingredients:

Directions:

Recipe Name:

Date:

Preparation Time:

Servings:

Special Note:

Ingredients:

Directions:

Recipe Name:

Date:

Preparation Time:

Servings:

Special Note:

Ingredients:

Directions:

Recipe Name:

Date:

Preparation Time:

Servings:

Special Note:

Ingredients:

Directions:

Recipe Name:

Date:

Preparation Time:

Servings:

Special Note:

Ingredients:

•
•
•
•
•
•
•
•
•
•
•
•
•
•
•
•
•
•
•
•

Directions:

Recipe Name:

Date:

Preparation Time:

Servings:

Special Note:

Ingredients:

Directions:

Recipe Name:

Date:

Preparation Time:

Servings:

Special Note:

Ingredients:

Directions:

Recipe Name:

Date:

Preparation Time:

Servings:

Special Note:

Ingredients:

-
-
-
-
-
-
-
-
-
-
-
-
-
-
-
-
-
-
-
-

Directions:

Recipe Name:

Date:

Preparation Time:

Servings:

Special Note:

Ingredients:

Directions:

Recipe Name:

Date:

Preparation Time:

Servings:

Special Note:

Ingredients:

Directions:

Recipe Name:

Date:

Preparation Time:

Servings:

Special Note:

Ingredients:

-
-
-
-
-
-
-
-
-
-
-
-
-
-
-
-
-
-
-
-

Directions:

Recipe Name:

Date:

Preparation Time:

Servings:

Special Note:

Ingredients:

Directions:

Recipe Name:

Date:

Preparation Time:

Servings:

Special Note:

Ingredients:

Directions:

Recipe Name:

Date:

Preparation Time:

Servings:

Special Note:

Ingredients:

Directions:

Recipe Name:

Date:

Preparation Time:

Servings:

Special Note:

Ingredients:

Directions:

Recipe Name:

Date:

Preparation Time:

Servings:

Special Note:

Ingredients:

Directions:

Recipe Name:

Date:

Preparation Time:

Servings:

Special Note:

Ingredients:

Directions:

Recipe Name:

Date:

Preparation Time:

Servings:

Special Note:

Ingredients:

Directions:

Recipe Name:

Date:

Preparation Time:

Servings:

Special Note:

Ingredients:

Directions:

Recipe Name:

Date:

Preparation Time:

Servings:

Special Note:

Ingredients:

Directions:

Recipe Name:

Date:

Preparation Time:

Servings:

Special Note:

Ingredients:

-
-
-
-
-
-
-
-
-
-
-
-
-
-
-
-
-
-
-
-

Directions:

Recipe Name:

Date:

Preparation Time:

Servings:

Special Note:

Ingredients:

Directions:

Recipe Name:

Date:

Preparation Time:

Servings:

Special Note:

Ingredients:

-
-
-
-
-
-
-
-
-
-
-
-
-
-
-
-
-
-
-
-

Directions:

Recipe Name:

Date:

Preparation Time:

Servings:

Special Note:

Ingredients:

-
-
-
-
-
-
-
-
-
-
-
-
-
-
-
-
-
-
-
-

Directions:

Recipe Name:

Date:

Preparation Time:

Servings:

Special Note:

Ingredients:

Directions:

Recipe Name:

Date:

Preparation Time:

Servings:

Special Note:

Ingredients:

-
-
-
-
-
-
-
-
-
-
-
-
-
-
-
-
-
-
-
-

Directions:

Recipe Name:

Date:

Preparation Time:

Servings:

Special Note:

Ingredients:

Directions:

Recipe Name:

Date:

Preparation Time:

Servings:

Special Note:

Ingredients:

Directions:

Recipe Name:

Date:

Preparation Time:

Servings:

Special Note:

Ingredients:

Directions:

Recipe Name:

Date:

Preparation Time:

Servings:

Special Note:

Ingredients:

Directions:

Recipe Name:

Date:

Preparation Time:

Servings:

Special Note:

Ingredients:

Directions:

Recipe Name:

Date:

Preparation Time:

Servings:

Special Note:

Ingredients:

Directions:

Recipe Name:

Date:

Preparation Time:

Servings:

Special Note:

Ingredients:

Directions:

Recipe Name:

Date:

Preparation Time:

Servings:

Special Note:

Ingredients:

Directions:

Recipe Name:

Date:

Preparation Time:

Servings:

Special Note:

Ingredients:

Directions:

Recipe Name:

Date:

Preparation Time:

Servings:

Special Note:

Ingredients:

Directions:

Recipe Name:

Date:

Preparation Time:

Servings:

Special Note:

Ingredients:

Directions:

Recipe Name:

Date:

Preparation Time:

Servings:

Special Note:

Ingredients:

-
-
-
-
-
-
-
-
-
-
-
-
-
-
-
-
-
-
-
-

Directions:

Recipe Name:

Date:

Preparation Time:

Servings:

Special Note:

Ingredients:

Directions:

Recipe Name:

Date:

Preparation Time:

Servings:

Special Note:

Ingredients:

Directions:

Recipe Name:

Date:

Preparation Time:

Servings:

Special Note:

Ingredients:

-
-
-
-
-
-
-
-
-
-
-
-
-
-
-
-
-
-
-
-

Directions:

Recipe Name:

Date:

Preparation Time:

Servings:

Special Note:

Ingredients:

-
-
-
-
-
-
-
-
-
-
-
-
-
-
-
-
-
-
-
-

Directions:

Recipe Name:

Date:

Preparation Time:

Servings:

Special Note:

Ingredients:

Directions:

Recipe Name:

Date:

Preparation Time:

Servings:

Special Note:

Ingredients:

-
-
-
-
-
-
-
-
-
-
-
-
-
-
-
-
-
-
-
-

Directions:

Recipe Name:

Date:

Preparation Time:

Servings:

Special Note:

Ingredients:

-
-
-
-
-
-
-
-
-
-
-
-
-
-
-
-
-
-
-
-

Directions:

Recipe Name:

Date:

Preparation Time:

Servings:

Special Note:

Ingredients:

-
-
-
-
-
-
-
-
-
-
-
-
-
-
-
-
-
-
-
-

Directions:

Recipe Name:

Date:

Preparation Time:

Servings:

Special Note:

Ingredients:

Directions:

Recipe Name:

Date:

Preparation Time:

Servings:

Special Note:

Ingredients:

Directions:

Recipe Name:

Date:

Preparation Time:

Servings:

Special Note:

Ingredients:

-
-
-
-
-
-
-
-
-
-
-
-
-
-
-
-
-
-
-
-

Directions:

www.ingramcontent.com/pod-product-compliance
Lightning Source LLC
LaVergne TN
LVHW082248150826
845677LV00009B/1571